A to Z Kenya

BY JUSTINE AND RON FONTES

children's press®

A Division of Scholastic Inc.
New York Toronto London Auckland Sydney
Mexico City New Delhi Hong Kong
Danbury, Connecticut

Consultant: Linda D. Bullock, Ph.D.
Series Design: Marie O'Neill
Photo Research: Candlepants Incorporated

The photos on the cover show a sunset over savannah (right), a giraffe (bottom right), a Masai girl (bottom left), and zebras drinking from a waterhole (left).

Photographs © 2003: Corbis Images: 6 right, 8 right (Paul Almasy), 24 right (Adrain Arbib), 18 right, 19 top left, 33 right (Yann Arthus-Bertrand), 29 (Jan Butchofsky-Houser), 14, 15 (Contemporary African Art Collection Limited), 13 bottom (Christopher Cormack), 4 center (Reinhard Eisele), 27 bottom (Stephen Frink), 10 (Michael S. Lewis), 28 bottom (Wally McNamee), 16 right (Richard T. Nowitz), 17, 33 left (Carl & Ann Purcell), 12 bottom, 16 left (Reuters NewMedia Inc.), 34 (Wendy Stone), 28 top (Liba Taylor), 12 top (The Purcell Team), 6 left, 32; Dembinsky Photo Assoc./Stan Osolinski: 38; Envision/Dennis Galante: 11; Getty Images/Digital Vision: 7; Lauré Communications/Jason Lauré: 26 top, 26 bottom, 36, 37; National Geographic Image Collection/Medford Taylor: 19 bottom; Photo Researchers, NY: 35 right (Jack Fields), 13 top (John Reader); PhotoDisc/Getty Images: cover top right (Amanda Clement), cover bottom right (Sami Sarkis), cover top left (Jeremy Woodhouse); PictureQuest/Carl & Ann Purcell/Words and Pictures: 18 left; Stone/Getty Images: 25 (Christopher Arnesen), 30 (Michael Busselle), cover bottom left (James Martin), 31 (Manoj Shah), 24 left (Art Wolfe); Taxi/Getty Images/Steve Bloom: 5 top; The Image Bank/Getty Images: 8 left (Grant V. Faint), 4 top, 4 bottom, 19 top right (Guido Alberto Rossi), 22, 23 (Paul Souders), 5 bottom (Art Wolfe), 9 right (Yellow Dog Productions); The Image Works: 9 left (Carol Beck & Angela Fisher/HAGA), 24 bottom (Richard Lord); Visuals Unlimited/Francis E. Caldwell: 35 left; Woodfin Camp & Associates/Betty Press: 27 top.

Library of Congress Cataloging-in-Publication Data

Fontes, Justine.
  Kenya / by Justine and Ron Fontes.
     p. cm. – (A to Z)
Includes bibliographical references and index.
Contents: Animals – Buildings – Cities – Dress – Exports – Food – Government – History – Important people – Jobs – Keepsakes – Land – Map – Nation – Only in Kenya – People – Question – Religion – School and sports – Transportation – Unusual places – Visiting the country – Window to the past – X-tra special things – Yearly festivals – Z.
  ISBN 0-516-24566-X (lib. bdg.)   0-516-26813-9 (pbk.)
1. Kenya–Juvenile literature. [1. Kenya.] I. Fontes, Ron. II. Title.
III. Series.
  DT433.522.F36 2003
  967.62'003–dc21

                              2003006008

1 2 3 4 5 6 7 8 9 10 R 12 11 10 09 08 07 06 05 04 03

Contents

Animals

Termites are less than
1 inch (2.5 cm) long,
but can build mounds
up to 20 feet (6 m) tall.

Kenya is alive with animals
of all shapes and sizes. There
are large animals like rhinos
and small ones like termites.

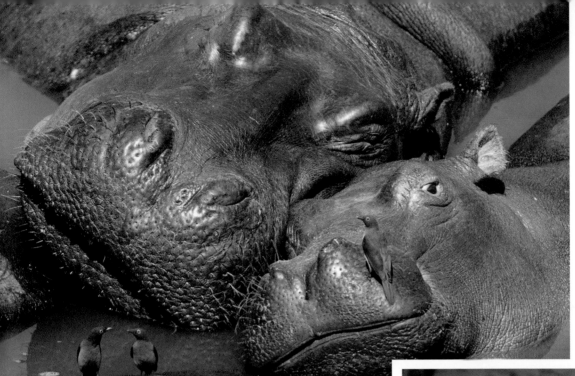

Baby hippos stay close to their mothers. That helps them stay safe from crocodiles that would eat them.

Impalas

The name **hippopotamus** means "river horse." That's because a hippo spends most of its day in the water. The hippo is the largest animal to live on land. It can weigh more than 8,000 pounds (3,629 kg).

Antelopes live in Kenya too. They are in the same family as cows. Bongos and impalas are antelopes. Impalas run and leap. They can leap 10 feet (3 m) off the ground in one jump.

Mnyama
(m-YAH-mah)
means animal

5

This is the McMillan Memorial Library. It was named after a farmer who came to Kenya in 1905.

Kenyatta Conference Center

Buildings

Nairobi (nigh-ROH-bee) is Kenya's capital. It is also the largest city. There are many modern buildings here. The tallest building in Nairobi is the Kenyatta Conference Center. From the top, visitors can see **Mt. Kilimanjaro**.

Nairobi

Cities

Nairobi is growing fast. More than one million people live there. Many work in factories and offices. Others work as tour guides.

Trains take visitors from Nairobi to Mombasa (mahm-BAH-suh). Mombasa is the second largest city in Kenya. Most of the city is on an island. You can use a ferry service or bridge to get to the mainland.

Some people also visit Lamu Island. Lamu is the oldest city in Kenya.

Schoolchildren

Dress

There are many different groups of people in Kenya. Many of them wear special clothing and jewelry.

In Kenya, many people wear cotton clothes that are comfortable in hot weather.

The Kikuyu (kye-KOO-yhoo), Luhya, Luo (luh-WOE) and Masai (mah-SIGH) are some of the groups that live in Kenya.

The color red is important to Masai people. Both men and women wear red clothing. Women wear colorful wraps called **kanga**. Men wear wraps called **kikoi**. The men also use red soil to color their hair.

Masai men and women cut their ear lobes to wear earrings. They also wear colorful beads.

Shuka

(sh-TOO-khah)
A Masai warrior's red cloak.

Coffee beans

Exports

Farming is important in Kenya. Kenyan farmers export, or sell some of what they grow to people in other countries. Two of Kenya's most important crops are tea and coffee.

Workers pick berries from the coffee plants. The berries are peeled to get the coffee beans inside. After the beans dry in the sun, they are loaded onto ships at Mombasa. From there, they travel around the world.

Kenyan farmers also export delicious nuts and fruits, like cashew nuts, pineapples, and different kinds of bananas.

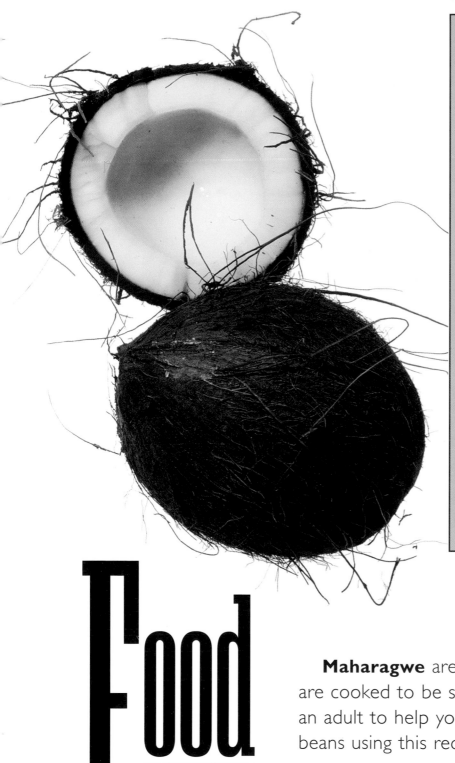

Kenya Maharagwe Recipe

WHAT YOU NEED:
- 1 pound of red beans
- 2 cups of coconut milk
- 2 to 4 tablespoons sugar
- 1/4 teaspoon ground cinnamon
- 1 teaspoon salt

HOW TO MAKE IT:
Wash the beans. Put them in a large cooking pot. Add water to boil. When the beans are almost cooked, add the milk, sugar, salt, and spices. Cook until the beans are soft. Top with coconut flakes. Serve with bread.

Food

Maharagwe are red beans. They are cooked to be spicy or sweet. Ask an adult to help you make some sweet beans using this recipe.

Jomo Kenyatta

Government

Kenya is a **republic**. That means the people vote for their leaders. Kenyans who are at least 18 years old vote every five years. They choose their president and most of the members of the National Assembly. People in the National Assembly make laws for the country.

Some leaders from the National Assembly help the president.

Kenya's first president was Jomo Kenyatta (JOH-moh ken-YAH-tuh). He became president in 1964, after Kenya became a free country.

Mwai Kibaki became Kenya's president in 2003.

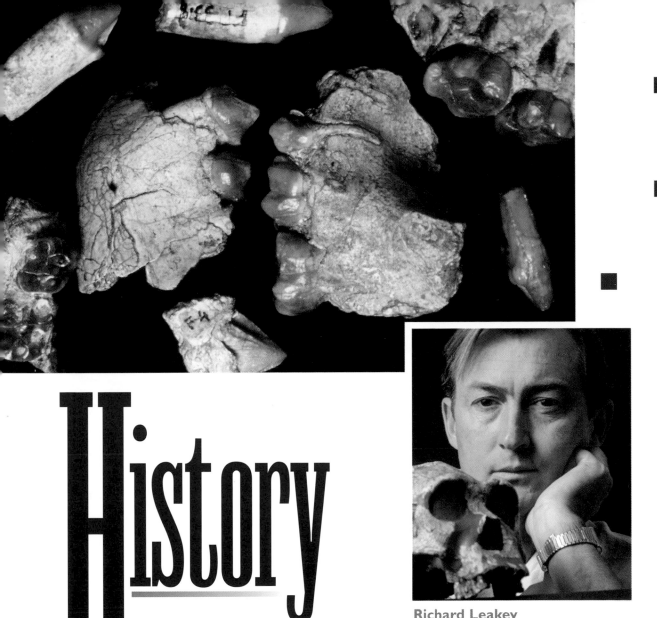

Richard Leakey

History

The first humans were found in the **Great Rift Valley** in Africa. **Scientists** think the first humans lived in Africa about two million years ago. Why do scientists think this? They have found important clues in Kenya.

Mary and Louis Leakey were scientists. They found very old bones, tools, and rock paintings.

Their son, Richard, also became a scientist. He and other Kenyan scientists have found more clues. In 1984, a human skeleton about 1,600,000 years old was found.

Porcupine, Elephant, Panther, and Gazelle, 1990

Important People

14

Taabu, 1992

Kivuthe mbuno

Kivuthi Mbuno is an important Kenyan artist. He uses ink, colored pencils, and special crayons to draw.

Before Kivuthi Mbuno became an artist, he worked as a cook on safaris. As he traveled through Africa, he learned more and more about the land, people, and animals. In his art he showed how people and animals lived together and survived. His large, colorful paintings tell stories of the Wakamba people. People in many countries have enjoyed Mbuno's art.

Msanii

(m-sahn-bee)
means artist.

15

Doctors and other scientists are working to help keep people in Kenya healthy.

These two young men show visitors their country. They are tour guides.

Jobs

Many Kenyans farm to feed their families. Some grow crops like corn. Others raise animals like cows and goats.

Some Kenyans are nomads. This means they move from place to place, looking for food and water.

Each year more people leave their farms. They move to towns and cities to find work. Some work in factories and offices. Others work in hospitals, schools, museums, hotels, and restaurants.

Keepsakes

Some shoppers like the colorful Masai beads. Others like Masai spears, shields, and masks.

If you like woven baskets, you can buy a **kiondo.**
You can find them all over Kenya. There are also many different kinds of wooden carvings of African animals and people to take back home.

Kenya's colorful cotton cloth is popular too. Some people like the kanga and kikois wraps that are made from the cloth.

Have you ever seen "elephant hair" bracelets? Some shops sell them. These bracelets aren't really made from elephant hair. They are made from grass, plastic, or metal. Some people believe the bracelets keep them safe.

17

Great Rift Valley

Land

Mlima

(ml-BEE-mah)
means mountain.

Kenya has sandy beaches, swamps, and small patches of rain forest too. However, most of Kenya's land is flat and dry.

Up to 2 million flamingoes gather at Lake Nakuru.

Some people go to see wild birds like pink flamingoes, pelicans, and storks. Look at this flamingo up close.

These flat lands are called **savannahs**. Zebras, buffaloes, giraffes, and elephants live on the savannahs. So do cheetahs, leopards, and lions.

Most of the people live in the **highlands**. The soil is good for farming since there is enough rain for crops to grow. Nairobi is in the highlands.

The Great Rift Valley cuts the highlands into east and west. Lake Turkana is in the north of the valley and volcanoes form islands in the lake.

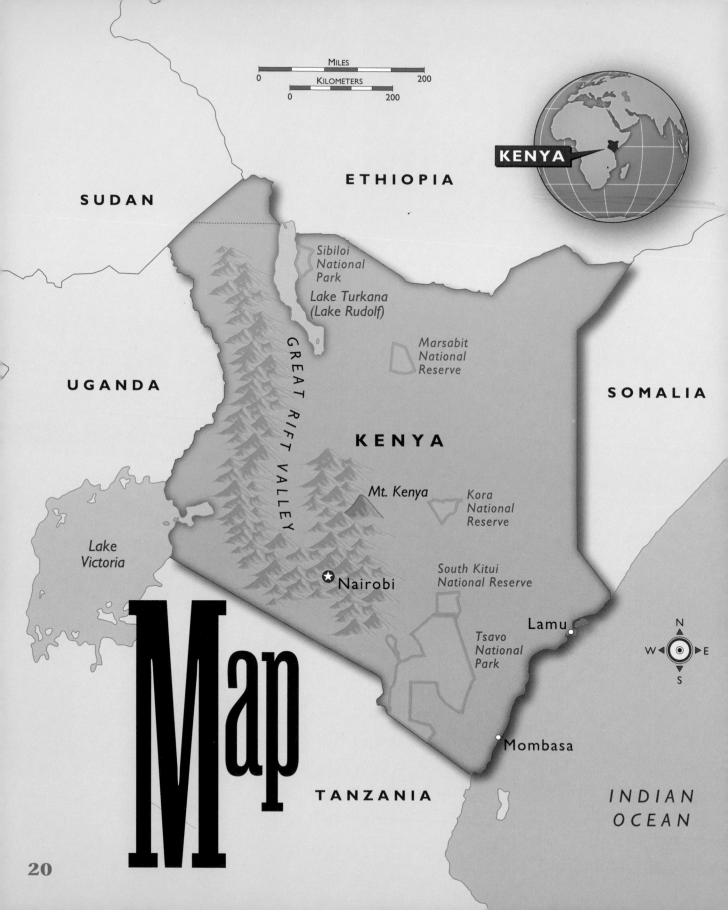

MILES

0   200

KILOMETERS

0   200

KENYA

SUDAN

ETHIOPIA

UGANDA

SOMALIA

Sibiloi National Park

Lake Turkana (Lake Rudolf)

Marsabit National Reserve

KENYA

GREAT RIFT VALLEY

Mt. Kenya

Kora National Reserve

Lake Victoria

★ Nairobi

South Kitui National Reserve

Lamu

Tsavo National Park

Mombasa

Map

N

W · E

S

TANZANIA

INDIAN OCEAN

ation

In 1895, Great Britain took over Kenya. Then in 1963, Kenya became free. The red stripe on the flag stands for their fight to be free.

There are two other stripes on Kenya's flag. One is black, and one is green. The black stripe stands for the people of Kenya. The green stripe stands for the land.

In the middle of the flag are a shield and two spears. These stand for the people's fight to stay free.

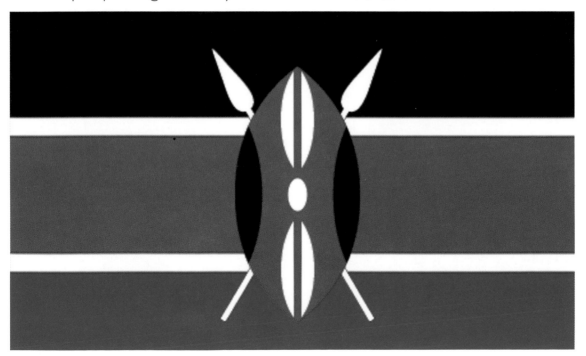

Only in Kenya

Kenya is one of the best places in the world for a **safari**. It has many safari parks, where visitors can see Africa's wild animals living free.

Visitors can ride in cars, on horses, walk, or float in hot air balloons to see the animals.

During the day, the sun is bright and hot. Animals rest in the shade of tall grasses and shrubs so it is hard to see them.

Early mornings and late afternoons are the best times to see animals. Hippos are very busy then. They yawn, snort, and come out of the water to eat grass.

On a Safari, you can come face to face with a cheetah.

23

People

There are more than 40 different groups of people in Kenya. Each group in Kenya has its own language. Sometimes, the groups have different ways of life, too.

Masai women dancing

The Kikuyu make up the largest group of people in Kenya. They live and work in cities. Others own large farms in the highlands.

They are part of a people called the Bantu. The Kamba, Luhya, and Kisii are also Bantu people.

The Luo and Kalenjin people are not Bantu people. They speak their own languages.

People in Kenya use Swahili, or Kiswahili, to speak to each other. People who go to school also learn English.

Question

What are the tallest animals on Earth?

Giraffes are! Giraffes can grow 18 feet (5 m) tall. Imagine three tall men standing on each other's shoulders. That's about how tall a giraffe is.

Giraffes also have very long tongues. They eat leaves from acacia (uh-KAY-shuh) and mimosa (mih-MOH-suh) trees. A long neck and tongue make it easier for a giraffe to eat leaves other animals can't reach.

Fun Fact:

A frightened giraffe can gallop up to 30 miles (48 km) per hour!

Religion

Muslims travel from all over Kenya to worship at the Mosque of Nairobi.

About half of the people who live in Kenya are Christians. A small number of Kenyans are Muslims and Hindus. Some people in Kenya practice old African religions.

There are hundreds of African religions. People who practice these religions believe in one god. Some also believe in many gods and spirits. The spirits are the ghosts of their **ancestors**. People pray to the gods and spirits for good health and help in their lives.

School & Sports

In Kenya there are not enough schools for everyone. Groups of people work together to start their own schools. These schools are called *harambee* schools. Harambee means "pulling together."

Many famous runners are from Kenya. Some run marathons, or long races. In 1999, men and women from Kenya won marathons in three different cities in Europe and the United States!

Transportation

Most people ride on buses to get around. There are buses that take people through the savannah to see Kenya's wild animals. There are also buses called matatus. **Matatus** are colorful. Some are dangerous because they carry too many people and go too fast.

In the cities, some people ride bicycles or take taxis. Very few people own their own cars, but trains are cheap and take people from city to city. Most roads in Kenya are not paved, which makes them hard to travel on.

Unusual Places

Lake Bogoria is in the Great Rift Valley. It has **hot springs** and **geysers**. At a hot spring, melted rock under the earth warms the water. Sometimes the hot water explodes out of the ground. Then it is called a geyser.

Large flocks of pink flamingoes live on the lake. The Greater Kudu lives here, too. It is a kind of antelope. It has four to ten stripes on its sides. Male kudus have twisted horns that can be 5 feet (1.5 m) long.

Fun Fact:

The hot springs in Lake Bogoria are hot enough to boil an egg!

Visiting the Country

One of the best ways to see Kenya is from the sky!

Floating in a hot air balloon is an exciting way to see Kenya. From the sky, people can see Kenya's wide **plains**. They can also see herds of animals and flocks of birds.

Safari balloons take off when the sun comes up. This is the cool part of the day. Riders fly above a national park.

One amazing sight to see is in the Masai Mara. Lions, buffaloes, elephants, leopards, and rhinos live here. Then each summer, large herds of **wildebeests** come into the park.

Masai warriors wore headdresses. Some were made from ostrich and eagle feathers.

Window to the Past

In the past, Masai boys grew up to be warriors. They raised cattle and moved from place to place.

Masai shields were made of painted antelope hide. The decorations showed a warrior's age and rank.

Some Masai celebrate by jump dancing. Young warriors try to jump the highest while singing.

Cattle have always been important to the Masai. Milk and cow blood were part of their diet.

To become a warrior, boys stole cattle from other Masai or killed a lion.

Many still raise cattle. They raise sheep, goats, and donkeys. Other Masai have built farms. Today, some Masai have given up their old ways. Some have moved to cities to go to school and work.

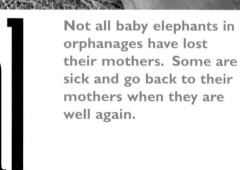

X-tra Special Things

Not all baby elephants in orphanages have lost their mothers. Some are sick and go back to their mothers when they are well again.

Where do baby elephants go, when they have no mothers? They go to an elephant **orphanage**.

Two baby elephants play in a mud bath to cool off.

A man carves animals out of ivory tusks.

For a long time, elephants were killed for their tusks. These are long teeth made from ivory. Elephants use them to dig for food and water. People sell the tusks for money.

Today, laws do not let hunters kill elephants for their tusks. Yet some hunters do it anyway. Sometimes the elephants they kill have babies. People rescue the babies and put them in orphanages until they are old enough to go back to the wild.

Tembo

(tsay-MNB-ho)
means elephant.

35

Independence Day Celebration

Yearly Festivals

December 12 is Independence Day in Kenya. This marks the day Kenya became a free country.

Different groups of people in Kenya have their own celebrations.
The Hindu are one group.

There are lots of things to do in Kenya all year round. There are dog shows and horse shows. There are fishing contests and polo matches.

For three days each October, people ride camels in a camel derby, or race. You don't have to own a camel to race. Anyone can join in the fun. Beginners go around the town of Maralal once. The course is about 7 miles (11 km) long.

For people who like to move faster, there are motorcycle and car races, too.

Zungu

Zungu means remarkable. Wild animals help make Kenya remarkable.

Some animals from Kenya such as lions, giraffes, elephants, and zebras live in zoos around the world.

Kenya has many national parks. It also has places where people care for animals. People there work hard to be sure Kenya will always have amazing animals.

People also visit Kenya to see animals in the wild. Will you?

■ Kiswahili and English Words

ancestor (**AN**-sess-tur) a family member who lived long ago

antelope (**AN**-tuh-lope) any of many fast, deerlike animals

geyser (**GYE**-zur) a hot spring that gushes a column of water

Great Rift Valley— an area of fertile, steep valleys in Eastern Africa formed by splits in the earth's crust

harambee (hah-**RRAHMB**-say) Kiswahili word for pulling together

harambee school— a school started by a community for its children

highland (**HYE**-luhnd) an area of mountains or hills

hippopotamus (hip-uh-**POT**-uh-muhss) a large African animal that lives near water

hot spring— a place where water heated by the earth's core rises to the surface

kanga (**KHAHN**-ngah) red wraps worn by Masai women

kikoi (khbe-**HO**-bee) red wraps worn by Masai men

kiondo (kh-bee-**HONE**-dho) a woven basket

maharagwe (mah-ah-rrah-**NG**-wsay) Kiswahili word for beans

matatu (mah-**TAH**-too) a brightly-painted mini-bus

mlima (ml-**BEE**-mah) Kiswahili word for hill or mountain

mosque (**MOSK**) a building where Muslims worship

msanii (m-**SAHN**-bee) Kiswahili word for artist, craftsperson, and inventor

mnyama (m-**YAH**-mah) an animal

orphanage (**OR**-fuh-nij)

plains (**PLANES**)—a flat, treeless country

republic (ri-**PUHB**-lik) a country run by representatives elected by the people

remarkable (ri-**MAR**-kuh-buhl)

safari (suh-**FAH**-ree) a trip, especially in Africa, to see wild animals

savannah (suh-**VAN**-uh) a flat, tropical grassland with few or no trees

scientist (**SYE**-uhn-tist) a person who studies science for a living

shuka (sh-**TOO**-khah) a Masai warrior's red cloak

wildebeest (**WIL**-duh-beest) an African antelope

zungu (z-**TOONG**-too) Kiswahili word for remarkable, special

■ Let's Explore More

Furaha Means Happy: A Book of Swahili Words by Ken Wilson-Max, Hyperion Press, 2000

Through Tsavo: A Story of an East African Savanna (The Nature Conservancy) by Paul Kratter, Soundprints Corp., 1998

Kenya (Globe-Trotters Club Series) by Sean McCollum, Carolrhoda Books, 1999

Websites

www.africaonline.com
News, games, and general information about Africa.

www.timeforkids.com
Search "Kenya" to find articles about a library that travels by camel and other amazing facts.

www.worldalmanacforkids.com/explore/nations/kenya.html
Learn lots about Kenya on this Web site.

Meet the Authors

JUSTINE & RON FONTES have written nearly 400 children's books together. Since 1988, they have published *critter news*, a free newsletter that keeps them in touch with publishers from their home in Maine.

The Fonteses have written many biographies and early readers, as well as historical novels and other books combining facts with stories. Their love of animals is expressed in the nature notes columns of *critter news*.

During his childhood in Tennessee, Ron was a member of the Junior Classical League and went on to tutor Latin students. At 16, Ron was drawing a science fiction comic strip for the local newspaper. A professional artist for 30 years, Ron has also been in theater as a costumer, makeup artist, and designer.

Justine was born in New York City and worked in publishing while earning a BA in English Literature Phi Beta Kappa from New York University. Thanks to her parents' love of travel, Justine visited most of Europe as a child, going as far north as Finland. During college, she spent time in France and Spain.